Pick Me! Pick Me!

Christine Woolf

WESTBOW·
PRESS
A DIVISION OF THOMAS NELSON
& ZONDERVAN

WestBow Press books may be ordered through booksellers or by contacting:

WestBow Press
A Division of Thomas Nelson & Zondervan
1663 Liberty Drive
Bloomington, IN 47403
www.westbowpress.com
1 (866) 928-1240

Because of the dynamic nature of the Internet, any web addresses or links contained in this book may have changed since publication and may no longer be valid. The views expressed in this work are solely those of the author and do not necessarily reflect the views of the publisher, and the publisher hereby disclaims any responsibility for them.

Any people depicted in stock imagery provided by Thinkstock are models, and such images are being used for illustrative purposes only.
Certain stock imagery © Thinkstock.

ISBN: 978-1-4908-4830-3 (sc)
ISBN: 978-1-4908-4831-0 (hc)
ISBN: 978-1-4908-4829-7 (e)

Library of Congress Control Number: 2014914580

Printed in the United States of America.

WestBow Press rev. date: 08/13/2014

To my husband, Steve, the love of my life,
who promised to help me be all God created me to be.

CONTENTS

PREFACE

One of the greatest challenges in our walk with the Lord will be to consent to His calling for our lives. We were indeed chosen before time to orchestrate works so amazing that people will be compelled to praise God when these works are witnessed.

The call has already been issued to every believer. Are you listening? Are you consenting to His call? How will you respond?

Proceed with caution. You have been picked, and this book will help you move forward.

INTRODUCTION

Wait! *Stop*! Don't skip the introduction!

Listen to this truth found in His letter—the Bible to us.

> Now to him who is able to do immeasurably
> more than all we ask or imagine, according
> to his power that is at work within us.
> (Ephesians 3:20)

The fact that you are reading a book that "I" wrote is proof of this very verse. There is no way on my own that I ever would have done this. Impossible. But with God all things are possible (Luke 18:27).

When I had my *"Aha!"* moment, I was scared, excited, embarrassed, determined, doubtful, faithful, bold, timid, and apprehensive. Simply put, I was a Dumpster of emotions.

When asked what I would do if I knew I could not fail, I replied, "Oh, I would write a book!" It just popped out of my mouth.

My head was screaming, "What are you saying?"

My emotions were commanding, "Get them back. Get those words back!"

But it was too late. The words were out, and I was awakened to His plan. Today, you are reading the very book I said I wanted to write. I fought to believe that His promises were for me. May I be living proof of God's promises.

My head is shaking even as I type those words.

This journey was such a battle and long walk, with seasons of doubting and disobedience.

However, today, as the verse clearly states, this work is according to *His* power that is at work within us.

This calling to be picked by God is exactly what you have longed for. I believe He is going to use what I have learned in the following pages to bring you revelation and encouragement to respond to that call.

If He can do a work in me, than I must encourage others to realize, He has great purpose and treasure for you.

I long for this book to be more than just a good read. I want it to be used by God to open your eyes to the truth of His Word. You were chosen.

A Chinese proverb says, "Tell them; they will forget. Show them; they will remember. Involve them; they will learn."

This book will require you to be involved, so that you can learn—learn His plan for your life.

You will have to commit to participating in this book. By that, I simply mean, please respond by writing what you hear the Holy Spirit speaking to you.

Please don't be that person who says yes and then doesn't do it. Please.

There is power in writing. Where would we be without scripture? I am thankful for writers. I hope you will be a writer.

So if you say to yourself, "Nah, I'm not a writer," I get that. Perhaps this book isn't for you. Very few respond to His call, God has asked me to write to the few. So, are you a part of the few?

Grab a pen. He has picked you. Let this book help you uncover the life Jesus died for you to have.

Humbled by my King that He chose an unskilled waitress, like me,

Christine Woolf

CHAPTER 1

CHOSEN

What does it mean to be called?

It's about drawing out that which you were created to do for His glory. You picked this book, but actually, *He* picked *you*. Who is He? He is God: God the Father, God the Son, and God the Holy Spirit. He has picked you that He may shine His glory through you. That concept alone is ethereal. That God would reveal Himself through people. Our struggle comes, when we realize that it is personal, He wants to shine through us.

Have you longed to be picked for something—anything? Perhaps, the lead in the school play, the sports team, the prom? How about a promotion or an acknowledgment of your hard work? What about marriage—have you longed for someone to choose you to be the object of his or her love? Perhaps you were orphaned and therefore have always had a "nonchosen" pain within you.

Maybe you have never been chosen for anything and have given up the hope of it. Perhaps you don't care anymore if you are ever picked. I wonder if you are already thinking this book doesn't pertain to you.

Don't go. God has chosen you.

The amazing truth is that you were chosen before the foundation of the world. It is my desire to communicate that as strongly as I can through this book.

Doesn't that last paragraph seem like a sci-fi statement? Doesn't it sound as if it is from out of this world? Truthfully, it *is* from another world—it is a heavenly kingdom.

> You did not choose me, but I chose you and appointed you, so that you might go and bear fruit-fruit that will last –so that whatever you ask in my name the Father will give you. (John 15:16)

May this verse be more than just words to you. The Bible says that His Word is alive and has the ability to go straight to the heart. You were chosen before the world began. It will take the Spirit of God to make that come to life for you.

The God of the universe longs for you to realize this truth. That is why He sent His Son Jesus down to earth— to reveal His plan. His plan involves you. He loved you so much that He sent His Son to make a way for you to come alive—really alive, beyond breathing, beyond existing.

He chose and appointed *you*. With a big sigh within me and the challenge before me, I will, with the help of the Holy Spirit, believe that by the end of this book, you will respond to the glorious call on your life. He has called you. Have you responded to that call?

I am reminded of a young man in the bible called Samuel, who heard God call him, however he failed twice to realize it was God calling. Samuel assumed it was Eli. Read what Eli told Samuel to do;

In 1 Samuel 3:9–10,

> "Go and lie down, and if he calls you, say,
> 'Speak, Lord, for your servant is listening.'"
> So Samuel went and lay down in his place.
> The Lord came and stood there, calling as
> at the other times, "Samuel! Samuel!" Then
> Samuel said, "Speak, for your servant is
> listening."

Are *you* listening? You have to listen with holy ears to what the Holy Spirit is saying. Read John 15:16 again with holy ears.

Did you hear it? "Much fruit, fruit that will last." Are you producing fruit that will outlive you? Will you have treasure when you get home to heaven? Is what currently consumes you devoted to His glory? This calling may interrupt your plans. It did for Abraham, Moses, the disciples and it will for you.

Let's begin.

You've been chosen. What are you going to with that? Do you hear Him call you? Are you listening? Write your response. Be real.

_____

_____

_____

_____

_____

CHAPTER 2

ALL ABOUT ME

The opening line of Rick Warren's bestselling book, *The Purpose Driven Life*, is "It's not about you." I remember this opening line almost ruining my vacation, the first time I read it.

We were on our way to the beach for a week's vacation. Anticipating the trip was almost as exciting as the trip itself. We had rented an oceanfront home in North Carolina. As we loaded everything into the minivan and began our twelve-hour drive, I made an announcement: "There will be food in the house that you are to make yourself. No fighting. Put your sunscreen on and let me be. This is my vacation too." My children were old enough to take care of themselves, lest you think I had bad parenting issues. "Oh, and one more thing: when I finally plant myself in my beach chair, it is all about me!" I was joking when I added the last part... *or was I?*

We arrived at the beach, and the salty air greeted us like an old family friend. The gentle breeze called us to unpack quickly and get at this thing called relaxation.

Without wasting any time, I unpacked the groceries and headed into the bedroom to begin Operation "It's All about Me." With sunsuit on, SPF 30 slathered all over, my favorite beach chair in hand, and a book my friend Michelle had given me, I headed through the mounds of soft white sand and focused on finding the perfect spot to plant myself.

I opened my beach chair, sat down, and could hardly take it all in. With the sun on my face, the breeze through my hair, and my toes in the sand, I began my vacation. I must have sat there for an hour trying to be all there. You know, the kind of feeling you get when the drive of life gets you to your destination, but the mental-emotional part of you fails to exit.

With a deep sigh, I ventured to read the book. I opened it and turned to the first page, and the first line read, "It's not about you."

"Are you kidding me?" I lamented. Had I not sunk my chair in the sand, I would have chucked that book to the depths of the ocean.

My husband Steve asked, "What's the matter?"

"I can't believe this book," I replied, and then I read the first line to him. Everyone laughed except me.

The Purpose Driven Life had invaded my space. I spent that week wrestling big questions. Although I came home from that vacation physically rested, I was mentally tired.

My life had great ups and downs. And there certainly have been people throughout time and space who have had their share of heart-wrenching trials. However, in my over-the-top selfish space of a vacation, this book invaded and dared to ask what my purpose was—that's all, nothing more.

There, in that moment, my purpose was to get a tan. Can you believe it? While many are without clean water, I was focused on a *tan*.

Don't get me wrong: I don't think there is a thing wrong with vacations or getting a tan. But this was "my week." I had waited three years for that vacation; I deserved it. People pull withdrawals from me day in and day out. That vacation was my "deposit" week. It was supposed to be about *me*!

A few months later, our church decided to use Rick's book for our spiritual renewal before Easter. Steve and I hosted a group at our home. It was the first night, and many were gathered in our living room. Steve led the study, and I took care of making sure the house was clean and there was candy in the candy dish.

Steve began the lesson and opened with that infamous line. I recalled my dislike for it. I blurted out, "You know, I've just got to ask. When will it be about me?" I don't think people expected the wife of the leader or the hostess to get so icky quite so quickly. There was an awkward silence.

Then a man gently broke the silence. "Chris, it was all about you on the cross."

"Oh."

I haven't been the same since that night.

I always knew God sent His Son to die for me, but I'm not sure I ever thought that it was just for me, that it was all about me, that it was a personal thing. I guess, looking back on it, I thought I was tagging along, so to speak.

The work of Calvary needs to go from general assumption to personal redemption. Once it does, you will have to respond to it. And the response is a life that acknowledges it has been "called" to something far greater than itself, a life that people will observe and have a immense desire to praise God as a result of witnessing.

So let me say to you the same thing that was said to me that night at Bible study. It was all about you on the cross. What have you done with Jesus death on the cross? Do you realize you have to do something with it? You must either accept the work of the cross or reject it. Perhaps this will be the first time you have thought about it and perhaps this will be the day you receive the forgiveness it offers. If so write your prayer of acceptance below.

If you have already embraced Calvary, how are you responding to it? Are you denying yourself and picking up your cross and are you following Him? Go ahead write about it below.

_____

_____

_____

_____

_____

CHAPTER 3

NEW LIFE

I have come that they may have life and
have it to the full.

—John 10:10

Jesus came to die on a cross for you so that you can
have eternal life. However, few have failed to receive the
second part of this verse. Life to the full—what does
that look like? I am beginning to understand that it
is living the life He *appointed* to me. Remember our
opening verse, John 15:16?

Pause and ask yourself, "Am I living this life?"

Stop and listen to your reply.

If I were speaking with you personally, I would really
emphasize this question to get a response. It's that
important.

Are you experiencing life to the full?

So many people give little thought to what they are doing. They are just trying to survive. God designed your life so that you could thrive in every situation, good or bad.

Imagine with me what the world would look like if every believer believed God had a plan for them. God would set this world ablaze with His glory working through our appointed lives. Satan does not want any praise going to God and certainly not because of your life. So he lies to us and we foolishly believe. He will tell us things, such as, "it is too late, you have messed up too bad or God is mad at you."

The Enemy cannot do one thing about the fact that you are saved. Because we tolerate the lies, he can and does do much with our quality of life. If we believe a lie as a truth, it has the effect of truth.

What lies do you believe regarding your life? Are you living the life that God has appointed you? If not, why not? The breakdown is in our belief and our failure to receive. In the chapters that follow, I will try to encourage you into believing truth that will break you free to be all that He has created you to be.

Jesus came that we might have life and to the full. Daily, I must ask myself: Am I living the life that He appointed me to have, and do I see lasting fruit? It is a daily choice to believe by faith that He is working His plan for my life. I do have to cooperate and walk in obedience.

This appointed life may be doing big things or little things great. Not all are appointed to become US presidents!

Is it possible to live your whole life possessing eternal life and not grasp the fullness this verse talks about? I think so. Many believe in God for their eternal salvation and that's where it ends. But "life to the full" rarely is possessed. Why? I think it is because people struggle to believe that God actually wants to use them. They look within themselves and see such brokenness that they reject God's calling.

God is not asking you to respond with anything in you. He is asking you to respond to Him alone.

Ask Moses, Abraham, Paul, even Peter. When God called them to be used by Him, they all responded with unbelief. Look at Peter's response in Luke 5:8 When Simon Peter saw this, he fell at Jesus knees and said "go away from me, Lord; I am a sinful man!

God is not calling to any ability in you, He is calling you to believe in His ability through you.

Is this calling so huge that I won't even want to do it? Am I going to be asked to lead millions from slavery, like Moses? Maybe. Whatever it is, it is fulfilling. Perhaps, you are already living it, you simply haven't embraced it. The enemy can blind you and rob you of your joy. Here is an example; being a stay-at-home mom. For many this is their calling, they just haven't embraced it, perhaps because at times it doesn't feel like it. It just seems custodial and unrewarding. Nothing like cleaning the house only to have it trashed the very next day. How can doing this stay at home mom thing bring God glory?

Someday we can ask Mary, the mother of Jesus that question, after all, the only thing she did was be Jesus' mom.

> If anyone acknowledges that Jesus is the Son of God, God lives in them and they in God. And so we know and rely on the love God has for us. (1 John 4:15–16)

Did you catch that in verse 16? We *know* and rely on the love God has for us.

We see, through Scripture, that we indeed can know. Would God love us and then fail to direct us in this appointed life? No, He would not. God will guide us. He is a shepherd and we are His sheep. He will tell us His plan for our lives, that is if we ask. Jeremiah 33:3 Call unto me and I will answer you and tell you great and unsearchable things you do not know. I pray that He awakens the Spirit within you.

I believe that living this appointed life is indeed fulfillment, life to the full.

The book of John states that Jesus' sheep know His voice and they will not follow another. My Shepherd's intent is to lead me in the path of this life. Why then would He not give assurance of the direction? A Shepherd leads; he does not say, "Figure it out."

I have come to realize He may lead us on roads that can sometimes threaten and frighten us. The roads can be lonely and hard. However, although the path may be difficult, it is always bringing about a greater good within us. James, the half brother of Jesus, spoke about this in James 1:4: "Let perseverance finish its work so that you may be mature and complete, not lacking anything." God's goal is not the destiny. God's goal is us. He shapes us to His image on the journey.

This life will often take us to places that are beyond our own natural abilities. This happens so that God gets all the glory.

When my faith engages with God's Word and I do what it says, then I will start producing fruit that will continue to produce and produce. Lasting fruit is full of seeds that produce more fruit. All of those fruits have seeds, which produce more fruit. You get the picture. The fact that you are reading this book is testimony to this truth.

If one person awakens to the call of God in his or her life as a result of this book, and then in turn that person ignites the Spirit within another, then I am producing fruit that lasts.

I am embarrassed at my disobedience, in that I took years to write this book. When I first heard His call, I laughed like Sarai in the Bible did when she heard God's messenger say she was going to have a baby in her old age. I did not laugh out loud, but I was laughing on the inside at the mere thought.

I remember the moment well. It caught me totally off guard.

Our church does a vacation Bible school (VBS) for children every summer. They also do an adult VBS at the same time, I was asked to lead it one year. A book was already chosen for me to use: *What's So Spiritual About Your Gift?* by Henry Blackaby.

The book asks a bold question, it's an often asked question, many have asked it "what would you do if you knew you could not fail?"

I asked most in the room what their answers were. As one would imagine, they were not eager to share out loud. With much encouragement, however, they did. As I proceeded, one person interrupted and asked me what I would do.

I shake my head when I remember. It snuck out of my heart and through my mouth like a cat waiting for the door to open. "I would write a book."

Oh my land! Did I just say that? Get it back, get it *back*!

My eyes must have been as big as saucers. I think I scared myself. I don't even remember the class's response. It was as if time stood still for a moment, I had no words.

I really just thought I was joking, but it wasn't funny, because those words coming out of my mouth opened the door to something that was tucked away for a very long time. It was as if I became aware of what I was supposed to do.

I would love to say I got up the next morning and began writing. But it was years of struggling to believe God would use me. I had such huge insecurities. "I mean, come on, God. I am the gal who was on national television and bought an *S* for a vowel on *Wheel of Fortune*. Certainly you don't mean me? A book?"

Yeah (sigh), He wasn't joking. And yes, you read that right. I was on *Wheel of Fortune* and did indeed ask to buy an *S* for a vowel. And yes, I know and knew that *S* is not and was not a vowel. You would have had to have been there. Clearly, I am no longer embarrassed... gah!

The concept of me writing a book would *not* go away. I wouldn't tell anyone about it. I was just too embarrassed. The thought that I had anything to say in book form was crazy.

Henry Blackaby said it all in his book, I didn't have anything to add.

As I surrendered to His plan, I began to realize I did have something to add. I could share the struggle I had gone through to believe He would use someone like me to reveal His goodness and glory. Perhaps I could encourage others who know they have some kind of wonderful deep down inside, who just needed some prompting. If I could grasp doing things way beyond myself, then others might be encouraged to do so too. I am praying that God will use what I have learned to encourage you to life—abundant, appointed life.

I would go to Christian bookstores for some literature and see the discount table. I would think, "If I wrote a book, it would go straight to the discount table."

And then I heard Him say, "Ouch."

I immediately knew I had hurt the Holy Spirit. I had grieved Him. It was at this point that I realized I wouldn't be the one writing this book. He would be. My job was to cooperate with His plan and not allow my unbelief to stop Him.

Do you realize that when we fail to believe, we grieve the Holy Spirit? Ouch.

On my own, I am absolutely nothing. I know that well, from my past, from the tapes in my head, and from my own mistakes. But God, through the power of His Holy Spirit living in me, can write a book.

I am laughing now too. Only this time, it is at what God *can do*, not at what I can't. We are all called to live a life that is full—full of God.

This question is not a new question. It's been asked by lots of people. Today, I believe God is asking

If you knew you could not fail, what would you do through the power of My Holy Spirit to bring Me glory?

It's important that you write your answer down.

_____

_____

_____

_____

_____

CHAPTER 4

SCAREDY-CAT

If you are like me, and struggle with first time obedience, you may not have written down the last thing I asked you to. Writing it down really is important. Obedience is essential to what God is calling you to do. If you didn't respond to the very first request, how will you fulfill it?

If you have not filled in your answer to the "what would you do" question, please go back and do it.

When you read those words on paper, what are your thoughts?

Our thoughts can paralyze us. What will people think? Who am I? Look at my past! I can't do this. I'm too old. I'm too young. That's ridiculous! The list is endless.

> As a man thinks in his heart, so is he.
> (Proverbs 23:7)

Are you what you think you are? In order to do the things God has called us to do, we have to change the way we think about ourselves.

We are products of our choices. Think about that for a minute. We are what we have chosen to be.

I know some will say, "I am what has been done to me." Actually, it's how we respond to what has been done to us that will direct our steps. Have bad things happened to you? You may need healing. Your past explains you, but it is not an excuse to spurn what God wants for you.

One of His names is Redeemer. You cannot do anything to change your past, but He can. Let the Redeemer heal your past so that you can move forward in the life He died for you to have.

We are what we choose to be. In His Word, it states, "I set before you life and death, choose life" (Deuteronomy 30:19).

I believe that God and His greatness trump our pasts so that we do *not* have to be paralyzed. I also believe that what we think about our pasts will determine our futures.

Words, memories, and experiences are powerful, to be sure. But make no mistake: they are not greater than our God. We must constantly remind ourselves that our

God is greater. We must choose to believe that God can and will redeem our pasts.

The story of David and Goliath is a great example of that. I am going to assume that you all know the Bible story. However, in the event that you do not, it is found in 1 Samuel 17.

The giant verbally abused the army of God for forty days! That is all he did. He talked harsh words. He *never* lifted finger toward them. Still, the armies of the most high God were paralyzed. Paralyzed. Why? Because they simply *believed* the threats of the enemy.

We, like those armies, do not walk in the fullness of God because we choose to believe the words that have been spoken over our own lives.

Day after day, there was no victory to report. I wonder how Saul felt when he asked why his army was so defeated and their reply was, "The giant said mean things about us." It would have been funny if it weren't so sad, and unfortunately the same is true for many of us. Words, they can be a killer.

Do you have words from the past that stop you from this thing you said you would do if you knew you could not fail? Words from family, friends, and even yourself? What are they? Listen, you have heard them your whole life, it's time to get them out, write them down and let

God have the last word. Write down the lies the enemy has whispered to you.

_____

_____

_____

_____

_____

Now honestly, do those words *really* have the power to stop you from doing what you know you would do if you could?

Sadly, the answer is yes! They do! Words stopped the armies of God, and they stop us. Thus we spend our lives not walking in the victory that Jesus died for us to have.

So what do we do about that? Can we do anything about that?

Yes. Believe. Believe that God's word is more true for you. Y-O-U. The Bible also says that He can make all things new (Revelation 21:5). Now, I choose to think that is for me!

There is power, holy, majestic power, when we dare to believe in God's Word instead of what we think about ourselves or what has been said over our lives.

I think of Ezekiel speaking the Word to those dead, dry bones. Those bones came to life when God breathed on them. The Word is the breath of God. Are you listening? God wants to breathe life into you. This thing that you would do if you knew you could not fail is about to come alive. Do you believe that? He is picking *you*!

In 1 Samuel 17, David rose to the challenge, totally unmoved by the giant's words because David knew what the giant was: an uncircumcised Philistine. That simply meant that God's promises were not for the giant; they were with David. David knew it well. David knew who the giant was and who God was. The living God was with David when he killed a bear, the living God was with him when he killed the lion, and the living God would be with him when he killed the giant.

Do you know that our God is *alive*? The same Spirit that raised Jesus from the dead is alive and well in Y-O-U?

Do you know who you are and who our God is? Really? Does your life look like the Israelite army's or like David's?

This is where we confess our sin of not believing God over the lies in our heads. We have grieved the Holy Spirit. Let's tell Him we are sorry. And lastly, ask for strength to believe His Word in your life more than man's words in your life. The fullness of your life depends on you believing this truth.

_____

_____

_____

_____

_____

CHAPTER 5

CAN'T BE RIGHT

I am envisioning that some of you are not grasping what is happening within you. You highly doubt that God would pick you to enact the grand desire that is in your heart. Let's see what God has to say about that in His Word.

> May He give you the desires of your heart
> and make all your plans succeed. (Psalm
> 20:4)

When you read this verse, what is your first thought? Doubt that this is for you? Or does it give you hope? Does the trail of your life give you no hope that this is true for you now?

We always struggle with God's blessings when it comes to us, don't we? We can believe in blessings for other people, but for ourselves? Nope. We doubt. "Why would God pick me?" Boy, if there was anyone who would have known about feeling like nobody would ever pick them, it was David.

In 1 Samuel 16, we read that when Samuel was sent by God to anoint the next king over Israel, even Jesse, David's dad, didn't consider David a good choice. (Thanks, Dad! Ouch.) Sometimes the deepest hurts are the one closest to us. The Bible goes on to say that God does not look at the outside appearance; He looks at the heart.

Maybe you too have been hurt by someone close like a parent. Maybe you're fighting feelings of abandonment just like David did. I am sorry that your earthly parents did not champion you the way they should have. I am so thankful that you have a heavenly Dad who is for you, not against you. He will never leave you. The plans He has for you are amazing.

You may be tempted to reject this plan because of a rejection you have experienced. Like David we must think more about what God thinks of us, then what anyone else in our sphere.

I spent years struggling to believe that I was to write a book of encouragement for others. I had to battle non verbal tapes that told me I never did anything worth writing about. Only to find I was actually walking in the very steps I was to write about. Perhaps like me you miss the fact that God wants to do through you things you have never done. It's a new thing.

Just as He chose David, God has chosen you. God has chosen *you*.

> Let your light so shine before men, that
> people may see your good works and glorify
> the Father. (Matthew 5:16)

According to this verse, what are you supposed to do? You are to *let* your light shine. You have God-given desires in your heart that you may be refusing to let shine, simply because you don't believe that God would use you to glorify His name.

Wrong. He would use you, and He does.

I speak throughout the United States. I face people every time I speak who have resistance to God's Word for their lives, either because they fail to realize that God loves them or because they can't believe it's true.

The Devil *cannot* do anything about the fact that you are indeed God's child. But the Enemy *can* get you to doubt it, and thus persuade you never to walk in the rich inheritance that is yours simply by believing.

> Praise be to the God and Father of our
> Lord, Jesus Christ, who has blessed us in
> the heavenly realms with every spiritual
> blessing in Christ. (Ephesians 1:3)

Does this text say, "He has blessed us with *some* spiritual blessings"? No. It says *every* spiritual blessing. All of God's blessings are yours. He has picked you as the object of His affection.

Don't reject Him, stop saying things like, "I can't believe it, or this can't be right."

Today would be a great day to simply receive all that He has for you. You are going to have to do this by faith; without faith, it's impossible to please Him.

Surrender to His plan for your life. Surrender to His love. Please write out your prayer of acceptance of all that God has for you.

_____

_____

_____

_____

_____

CHAPTER 6

ON SECOND THOUGHT

Are you an educator by profession? Perhaps you have taught Sunday school? I love when the younger children are so eager to be picked. I have to chuckle at the thought that when you merely begin to ask for a volunteer, they raise their little hands without even knowing what they are volunteering for. "Ooh, ooh, please, please pick me, pick me!"

I sometimes like to pick a child and say, "Great! Thanks for volunteering to clean the bathroom."

To which I get the invariable response, "Hey, wait a minute! I'm not doing that!" Kids, they truly just want to be "picked."

Are you like those precious little ones having second thoughts about being picked? Perhaps the Holy Spirit has brought you to a place of acceptance, and now you are going to have to actually *do* this thing. Yep, that's how God works—*through* people.

I remember well when I gave my answer to the question about what I would do if I knew I couldn't fail. I said, "I would write a book." I never thought in a million years that I would. It was just a far-fetched, fun thing to dream.

As I sit here looking at this computer screen, I am in awe that I am doing this. There is certain awkwardness when you go forward with your desire. I feel kind of funny.

I guess it really doesn't matter what I feel; it matters what I know. I know that God, who began a good work in me, will help me complete it. And that means He will help with everything in between the desire and the book you're holding now. For that, I am so thankful.

On my own, I can do nothing. If He can use me, He can use you. You are just going to have to take my word on that one.

What you need to know is that from the time I answered that question to the time I actually started writing, there were years of unbelief. "God, you have the wrong girl for this assignment." It wasn't funny anymore.

I was faced with having to give an answer to His call. I never responded with a no. However, I never said yes either. I told God over and over, "I can't do this. Who am I to write a book?" It would be one really big paragraph,

I thought. Perhaps a really big run-on-and-off-the-paper sentence!

I think of how Moses responded when God called him. Mo came up with every excuse you could think of. God had a solution for every excuse, none of which convinced Moses. They went back and forth. Finally it just angered God.

And *that* is exactly what I didn't want to do—anger God. I tried His patience; I'm sure of it. I kept saying, "I'm doing it" as I wrote a little here, a little there.

That didn't change until I was reminded about Abraham, the part where God told him to circumcise himself and his household. The Bible says that he got up and did it *immediately*.

Can you imagine? Circumcision? Good night!

If Abraham gave God immediate obedience with that act, what in the world was I dragging my feet for? I then immediately got serious. But sadly, "immediately" getting serious took five more years. Oh, it pains me to write that.

The purpose of this book isn't to make my name famous. It's about making His name famous. Through my mistakes, I learned just how patient He is because I experienced His nature and attribute of patience. I had always known that it was a characteristic of His, but it wasn't until He called me to write this book that I grasped just how patient He is.

Are you struggling with immediate obedience? Do you feel like you are making God mad? Like He's ticked off at you? Do you feel like you disappoint Him?

Read this most comforting verse:

> And He passed in front of Moses, proclaiming, "The LORD, the LORD, the compassionate and gracious God, slow to anger, abounding in love and faithfulness." (Exodus 34:6)

Really slow—five years slow. Big sigh. Thank You, God. Thank You. I am so glad that our heavenly Father is slow to anger.

As a little girl, I remember asking my dad if he loved me. He would answer, "When you listen." Yea, often that was his response. I really had to learn God is not like my earthly dad.

Today, I have experienced God's love for me even when I do not listen. He knows that the voices of the past get in the way. He is patient and kind, not easily angered. We must *experience* our heavenly Father's love; it is nothing like that of our earthly father.

You may have had a wonderful relationship with your earthly dad. That is such a gift. However, it will still limit you if you think that what you experienced with your earthly dad is all that your heavenly Dad is capable of. He is so much more than that. You must learn who He is. The Bible is clear about that. Knowing who He is and experiencing who He is are two different things.

How about you? Have you experienced the patient God of the Bible? Please don't use His patience as an excuse not to step out and begin this journey. That just isn't nice. He loves us so much; why would we try Him by not giving Him immediate obedience? Move out of your place this day and follow the Holy Spirit.

How long has it been for you? Do you think God's love expires? It has no expiration date. It is still good and it is still for you. He is compassionate and gracious, slow to anger, abounding in love. He is so faithful, even when we are not. So great is His faithfulness.

Do you need prayer for your disobedience? Do you want to be like Abraham and act immediately?

> Father God, I know I am not alone with this struggle. Will you equip the person reading this and grant that person strength and courage to go immediately and be obedient? Jesus, you were obedient to the point of death on a cross. Help us be like you. Thank You, Jesus, for letting us

use Your name. Father, we are coming to
You in Jesus' name—He sent us.

Now you pray. Tell Him what you need help with.

_____

_____

_____

_____

_____

CHAPTER 7

TOO GOOD TO BE TRUE

Have you ever become overwhelmed by God's goodness in your life?

There have been times in my life when I have been awakened to His goodness and I could barely take it in. I am reminded of a story about Peter. He felt that way when he caught all those fish, right before Jesus called him to follow Him (Luke 5).

God's favor and goodness bestowed on Peter were more than he could take in. He told Jesus to get away from him, because he was "unclean." This happened after Peter caught the biggest catch of his life. God's goodness can be so overwhelming; we can be tempted to shun it. I am wondering if you too struggle to receive His goodness as the Holy Spirit awakens you to the fact that He wants to work through you. It's my prayer that He does indeed awaken you. When He does, be careful not to shun Him.

I have felt like that on many occasions. I find myself asking, "Why are you so good to me?" His abundance toward me is great. I start to think about things like the fact that half the world doesn't have clean drinking water, yet I drink freely whenever I want without worry of diease. I have so much money that it is even in the ashtray of my car! My attic is full, my basement is full, my garage is full of stuff that I haven't used in years. I am overwhelmed with the stuff of life. Don't even get me started on how many shoes this household has. Why does God bless me so when others have nothing? I am humbled.

And then I think about the fact that Jesus died for me, a sinner, and has given me eternal life, so undeserved. I am overwhelmed by His love and goodness. Like Peter, I am unable to bow low enough because of all His blessing.

David felt that way. He wrote of it in a few of the psalms. Over and over again, David asked God, "Who are we that You even think of us and care for us?" (Psalm 8:3-4). Even David, a man after God's own heart, struggled with God's pursuit of him.

Regardless of how we feel, the fact remains that we are the apple of His eye. Do you believe that for your life? Do you believe that He is purposeful toward you? That He desires to reveal Himself to you and has a great plan for your life? Do you believe that the plans He has for you are good?

Are you overwhelmed? God's goodness will do that.

You are going to need to do something with this blessing once you adapt to His call. You will need to engage your faith in order to move.

This life, that He calls us to can only be traveled by *faith*. Let me say it again. Faith is the *only* way. It is by faith we are saved. And it will be by faith that we live this life.

As I have walked with this faith, I am more aware each day of His goodness, the tapes from the past want me to push God away. When I receive all that He died for me to have, I think God delights in that. God is a giver, He gave His only Son. He loves children who receive. Have you ever given a gift that someone struggled to receive. They will say things like, "you shouldn't have", or "oh, why did you do this?. But give a 6 year old a gift and you will hear "oh wow!" and hopefully they will say "thank you!" We have to have child like faith.

Older people struggle to receive for many reasons, one of them is they don't think they deserve it. When you read that God wants to do amazing works through you, do you think you don't deserve that task?

Let's talk about the past, because when we think about moving ahead in this venture, the Enemy will try to stop us by reminding us of our pasts. It is a great tool of his, and it is effective; that is why he uses it.

When you drive a car the windshield is big because you are moving forward, and the windshield is in front. What is behind is important, but not as important as where you are heading.

No one drives looking through the rearview mirror. That mirror is small—for glances, to give us information. The rear is not the direction we are going.

Our pasts are our testimony of God's grace. The past does not define us. God defines us and declares us good because of the blood of Jesus. Nothing can stand against us, and that includes our pasts. We must press forward, focused on the Author and Finisher of our faith.

With each step you take, you must put up your shield of faith and divert the fiery darts that threaten to stop you. God is with you and for you. He is sufficient.

God told Moses that He would go with him, Moses wanted more, he wanted to take his brother, Aaron. It seemed that Moses was so insecure within himself that even God was not enough.

You and I have a chance to please God by believing that He is more than enough, that He is more than capable of doing great things in us and through us. God wants to use you to do great things. We have a choice to make: we can choose to believe all of God's Word for our lives, or we can choose not to. God says "I put before you life and death, choose life" (Deuteronomy 30:19).

Again, write a prayer of surrender and belief. Die daily to unbelief. Give Him all your excuses why He can't. Give Him your past, your failures, your faults–all of it. Then receive all His goodness. What a great trade.

_____

_____

_____

_____

_____

CHAPTER 8

DOUBT KILLS

Doubt kills more dreams than failure ever has.

You just gave Him all your failures and doubts in the previous chapter. Be aware that the Enemy will come back at a more opportune time. The Enemy did this to Jesus when he tempted Him for forty days, and he will do it to you too. He will not give up until he is successful in getting you to doubt God. We must be aware of his schemes and be prepared with the full armor of God. If we hold up our shields of faith, we will be able to put out every fiery dart.

The power of believing can make us unstoppable. Let me be clear it is Who we believe in that makes us unstoppable. It will only take our latest failure to remind us of all we cannot do. Our belief must be in someone greater than ourselves, someone victorious, like Jesus, who defeated everything, including death.

We need to settle once and for all that God is *for* us and stop the teeter-tottering back and forth, getting nowhere.

It may seem that I am belaboring this doubt-belief thing. If I am sounding redundant, I apologize, however it is the key that unlocks the impossible. We fix our eyes on Jesus the author and finisher of our faith.

I sense there is a person whose calling is so big, it's frightening. I want to fan the flame that is within them from the winds of the past that would blow it out. Doubt will do that. If you are gung-ho about this calling, be patient with me. There are still a few who are thinking, "This is crazy. I can't believe God would call me to do this thing."

If your faith is truly is in God—and you know that you can do all things through Christ—then proceed.

But if you aren't there yet and you keep looking within yourself, then I want to encourage you to put your faith in God.

Without faith, it is impossible.

I wonder if you are like me and responded as I would have when I first read that statement. "Yeah, yeah. I know. Faith, gotta have faith."

Do you have faith? Do you need more? Do you want more? Without faith, it is impossible to please God. Impossible.

Impossible. If you are being honest with yourself and you find doubt, you must confess it and allow God to forgive and strengthen you in your inner man. You are going to have to trust Him.

For example, I am writing this book with very little faith. I find nothing within me that feels like I can. I hear Him say, "Keep going". Let me be clear, I want to, I just feel incredibly incapable.

I look in my backpack as I wander this journey and see that my supply of faith is little.

I am comforted by Jesus' words that if I have a mustard seed's worth of faith, I can move mountains. I've got that. As I read His Word, my faith grows. If you find yourself needing your faith to grow, get into His Word. It is a hospital for weak faith.

Rick Sams, my pastor, says that success will be hearing God say to him at the end of his life, "Well done, good and faithful servant." I agree with him. Success is not what I accomplish; it is what He accomplishes in me, because I believe. He who began a good work in me is faithful to complete it. But in order for any of this to happen, I have to believe it!

If I can put my foot on a solid surface, if I know something for sure, then no faith at all is required. Walking by faith, the road will be invisible to me.

If I say that I did this, then I get the credit. If I know where I am going and I know what I am capable of, then I will receive the glory and not God. He will share His glory with no one. If I am out of my comfort zone and walk victoriously, then God gets the glory.

> Let your light shine before men, that they will see your good works and give God glory. (Matthew 5:16)

According to this verse, what are we to *let* shine? Who is the light? The answer is Jesus. Are you *letting* Jesus shine through you? Or do you think the goal is for *you* to shine? Will you simply let Him shine by believing His Word is true for your life?

I am not asking you if you are able. When God says, "Well done, good and faithful servant," He isn't saying, "Well done, very able servant." The Word says good and *faithful*.

With God, all things are possible. Do you believe that?

Once you hear the call on your life, you will face many battles of doubt. This book is meant to encourage you to believe He wants to use you. The Word will carry you through.

I am living proof. Are you living proof?

I pray that there is no doubt in you right now. It kills, just ask Eve.

Your biggest battle will not be the calling, it will be, believing God's word is true for you. Choose again this day to believe that His Word is personal. It is true today and tomorrow and the day after that. Remember, His faithfulness is greater than your ability to believe. Isn't He just awesome?

One more time, is there any speck of doubt? It's like when the surgeon comes out from surgery and says, we got 90% of the cancer. That's not acceptable, we know it has potential to grow and eventually kill. So can doubt, it can kill His plan for you.

Be still and listen to the Holy Spirit, ask Him to reveal any doubts you may have tucked away in the depths of your heart. Then ask God to replace them with faith.... rooted in Him. Use the space to write about the 10% you can't seem to get rid of. Lastly and most importantly write the scripture He shows you to replace that particular doubt with.

_____

_____

_____

_____

_____

CHAPTER 9

I HAVE NO CLUE

Some of you are actually hearing a call on your life. You may have known it all along and are encouraged by this book to act upon it. Others may be very frustrated. You have no clue what you would do.

In chapter 13, there is a map to help you find where you are. It is brilliantly titled "Map." You may want to glance at it now. Once you realize where you are, you can proceed with some clarity.

I talk about it later in that chapter, but the purpose of the map is to equip you to pray.

It's very possible that you will need to spend time in prayer about your calling, seeking His face. You simply aren't on the map...yet. And frankly, it could take a while. Don't be discouraged He definitely has works for you. And please do not walk away from this. I liken it to just finding out you are pregnant. You don[t look like it, feel like it and they is no evidence other then the test

44

results that you are. You don't know yet if it is a boy or a girl...or twins!

I have prayed Paul's prayer over the ones who may be struggling. I have prayed that your eyes be opened.

> I pray also that the eyes of your heart may be enlightened in order that you may know the hope to which he has called you, the riches of his glorious inheritance in the saints, and his incomparably great power for us who believe. (Ephesians 1:18–19)

Let's look at Moses, he was born a Hebrew and raised an Egyptian. He committed murder while in Pharaoh's family, fled to Midian, and married a Midianite. I would guess he struggled to know just who he was, let alone what he was called to do.

Moses was herding his father-in-law's sheep when God called him to do this amazing thing on behalf of His people. And it involved going back to the very place and palace Moses had fled so many years before.

You may want to read about it in Exodus 3; it continues through Exodus 4.

If I were to sit down and talk with Moses while he was out in the desert shepherding and ask, "Now Mo, what would you do for God's glory if you knew you would not fail?" I'm not sure he could readily answer. It's a big question. But God called through a burning bush, let's read it;

> There the angel of the LORD appeared to
> him in flames of fire from within a bush.
> Moses saw that though the bush was on
> fire it did not burn up. So Moses thought,
> "I will go over and see this strange sight-
> why the bush does not burn up."
>
> (Exodus 3:2-3)

Burning bush, waitress from Ohio? Same thing. God speaks through willing vessels for His glory.

Oh, I am sure Moses wasn't fulfilled herding his father-in-law's sheep. I am guessing, based on his past, he knew he was destined for more. The rubble of his life was trying to bury it. Until one day in the middle of a desert, God called.

There had to have been a deeply embedded desire in Moses to do what God was asking of him. Those mistakes from his past were big mistakes; after all, he had killed someone. That act may have haunted him into thinking he would never be anything other than a shepherd.

I think God spoke to the passion that had once been a flame in Moses. Moses had a passion to see his people be free. He chose to take matters into his own hands. He murdered. Moses failed to see the bigger picture, that he was in position to be a leader to free them right there in the palace. We will never know if God's plan all along was for Moses to take Pharaoh's place and free the Israelites more simply.

Maybe you are like Moses. You had a passion for something, and it failed—or you failed, or someone failed. God wants to resurrect it. What thing? That thing that died years ago and has been in the grave, that forgotten thing.

Are you getting nervous? Am I hitting a nerve? Do you want me to stop? You can stop, you know. You can put the book down and go back to herding your father-in-law's sheep, palace boy.

> If you belong to Christ, then you are Abraham's seed, and heirs according to the promise. (Galatians 3:29)

God is not going to force you to take hold of something He sent His Son to die for. You freely received the gift of salvation; you did nothing to earn it. You have by this act become a coheir with Christ. It is God's promise that makes this happen, not your victories or failures.

So it is with the lives we live on this earth, by His promises. He is really good at bringing dead things to life. You will have to cooperate with His plan to make this happen.

I told you it was big. You are going to have to depend 100 percent on God.

Uh-oh… we have a pulse.

This chapter was for all those like Moses out there, and this verse is just for you.

> And God said, "I will be with you. And this will be the sign to you that it is I who have sent you: When you have brought the people out of Egypt, you will worship God on this mountain." (Exodus 3:12 NIV)

What is the Holy Spirit saying to you?

_____

_____

_____

_____

_____

CHAPTER 10

THIS IS CRAZY

From that last chapter, did you hear anything? A whisper? A hint? Or does what you came up with just sound crazy?

Oh, how I understand! You are reading my crazy! Look at me—I am writing a book! *Crazy*!

When God choose Moses to go to Pharaoh, Moses had to have thought God was off His rocker. I mean, come on! When Moses last saw Pharaoh, they hadn't parted on good terms. And now God wanted Moses to go back and ask for all the people to be released. "Are you kidding God? Me?"

"Tell him I Am sent you."

"Well now, doesn't that make it better? Who? I Am? What in the world is that ? I Am... I am what?"

God's name I Aᴍ came to mean everything. It was Jesus standing before Pilate and declaring that He was the I Aᴍ that got Him crucified. There was no way Moses could have understood all that God would do with that name. Suffice it to say that Moses' obedience despite his strong reluctance proved favorable for millions upon millions.

We cannot fully understand what God will do with our obedience that is fueled by faith. God is pleased by our faith in His Word.

> Then I heard the voice of the Lord saying, "Whom shall I send? And who will go for us?" And I said, "Here am I. Send me!" (Isaiah 6:8)

I love this verse because God is just asking a question; it is not directed *at* Isaiah. God is merely calling out, "Who will go?"

Isaiah responds, "Send *me!*"

The Holy Spirit is calling out for us to believe that we serve a God who *can* and *will* do amazing things through His people, if only one of those people would dare to believe.

I know that it may seem crazy. Who would ever believe you?

God does! If you respond to His call and yield yourself to His Holy Spirit, people will see your good works and give God glory. There is nothing sweeter than being at the very core of what you were created for, which is causing your life to impact others to praise God. What a calling!

Moses made God angry by constantly asking God to let someone else do it. Don't we do that? We might not say no to God. We just keep making excuses why we think God has chosen the wrong person. God said to Moses, "I will go with you." But for whatever reason, Moses wasn't satisfied with just God. Yikes!

Don't be so quick to judge Moses. Don't we do the same thing? You and God—no one else, no brothers, no friends, just God—and we struggle to believe that is enough. If it were easy, everyone would be doing it. But God calls us to do things that seem hard. And sometimes the hardest thing is to do it alone—*with* God.

If God be for us, who can be against us? Sure, sounds good, until the tough and rough stuff starts to happen. When we start to act upon our calling and people start asking questions, we may suddenly delay our reply and long for someone to come alongside us to encourage us. But what if no one does? Is God alone enough?

You are going to have to know that you know He is calling you. Then *expect* bumps and power through them. Just don't be surprised if you are your own biggest bump in the road.

God is for you; nothing shall stand in your way. May He be more than enough for you when people think you're crazy.

Also, be prepared. Your family might be your loudest naysayers. Look up what Jesus' family thought about Him in Mark 3:21. Certainly if they thought that about Jesus, then rest assured they will think that about the Jesus in you.

I wish I could hear everyone's responses to the last chapter. I think it's exciting when God moves and His people believe.

Go ahead and pour out all your fears and concerns, Moses did, but unlike Moses, we will acknowledge by faith that He is enough. It's okay to be afraid. Remember perfect love. His love casts out all fear. May your fear be turned to excitement!

What are some things you think people will say when they hear about what you want to do?

_____

_____

_____

_____

_____

CHAPTER 11

OIL

When our family sets out for vacation, one of the things on my to-do list is to service the car before we go. I get the fill the tank with gas, sweep it out and change the oil.

Without oil, a car cannot run very long. It starts grinding on all its parts. Like the car, you need oil to get to your destination. The oil I am referring to is the anointing of the Holy Spirit, which is often referred to as oil in Scripture.

> The Spirit of the Lord is upon me, because he hath anointed me to preach the gospel to the poor; he hath sent me to heal the brokenhearted, to preach deliverance to the captives, and recovering of sight to the blind, to set at liberty them that are bruised. (Luke 4:18)

Can you imagine if the above job description was yours? To heal broken hearts and set captives free? Give sight to the blind? Yikes! Yet Jesus was anointed to do all of this and more.

God anointed Jesus to preach the gospel, and He did it by His Holy Spirit.

Just like Jesus was equipped for His purpose, so are you. The same Spirit that raised Jesus from the dead is alive and well in you. It is important that you grasp this. Otherwise you are going to try and do this work in your own strength, and that is far from enough strength for what He is calling you to do. He is calling you to do something you cannot do on your own. This is so big that if God doesn't show up, it will not happen.

Faith will drive this mission. Apart from God, we can do nothing. We must fully comprehend that it is all God from beginning to end. This fundamental truth will give you courage to agree to and proceed with His plan. Again, I'll remind you, your assignment is simply to believe that His Word is true for you. You simply believe.

Certainly, there has to be more than just belief or nothing will get done. Let's establish the kind of belief I am talking about. If I believe I can play the piano, and I do not take lessons or practice, then what good is my belief? It's useless. Now, imagine I believe I can play the piano *and* I take lessons and practice. What do you think of my belief then?

God needs us to be doers of the Word, not just hearers. This truth comes to us in James 1:22. James was the half brother of Jesus. He of all the people who wrote the books of the Bible is the one who could have told us what Jesus was like as a child. I find that interesting. Do you have a brother? If so, can you see him as the Messiah? James couldn't either, not until after the resurrection. James was living with the Messiah and in the midst of living with Him failed to grasp who He was.

So, when reading the book of James, consider that it comes through the pen of one who was awakened to the truth of his half brother. I read the book of James and I hear a holy fire in his penmanship. James tells us it is not enough to hear; you must do what you hear.

It may seem like I am contradicting myself. First I said God will do it through you, and then I said you must be the doer. Which is it? Both. It is in your believing that you will create the doing. Your work is to believe, then to do what He shows you. He will give you grace and power to do it. He will anoint you to do it.

This kind of action-believing is fundamental to walking in the fullness that God has called you to. Here is an example. Let's use my life, God told me to write a book. First, I took years to believe—years, I tell ya. Not only did I not tell anyone, I didn't write anything either.

After years of wrestling with God over this calling, I began to be a doer after He gave me the title *Pick Me! Pick Me!*

I started writing down everything that happened every time I sensed that He had picked me. I have pages upon pages of these events. I thought that the book would be a collection of anecdotes about these encounters.

As I wrote, He guided my steps to write about embracing the calling of being picked. Honestly, this book doesn't look a thing like I thought it would. Once I started moving, He started directing.

I have written things and then thought, "What in the world was I thinking? That makes no sense!" But I refused to give up. I worked my way through this with His help. As I write, I do not know what will become of this book. I don't even have the financial resources to print it (yet!).

In the meantime, I just do the next step. That is easy. I can do the next step. And so can you.

The Holy Spirit is the one who will work through you. You must cooperate. When you look to yourself, you will see all your inadequacies, just like I do. It is then that you will be tempted to stop. In order to have victory, you will have to walk by your faith and believe, just like a pilot is flies by his instruments to navigate through a storm.

Yes, you will appear "weird." Most likely you will hear yourself say, "What do I think I am doing?" You will be tempted to quit. So be on the lookout for self-defeating talk.

Speak the Word to yourself. Out loud is best. Truly, nothing is more powerful than His Word being spoken over your life. The Bible tells us that Ezekiel spoke the Word to the dead, dry bones and they came to life. The power of God's Word operating in your life is truly amazing.

This is how you move: you take a step. His Word is a lamp unto your feet. We walk by faith. The flame on those oil lamps gives enough light for the next step only. Think about that. You will only see the next step.

The Holy Spirit is the oil that greases all the moving parts. There will be an ease in your movement, just enough for the next step.

Abraham was called to a place he did not know. When I think about that, I imagine the conversation between him and Sarah. Sarah must have thought Abraham was crazy. "What do you mean, you don't know where we are going? Do you expect me to pack up everything we have and just start walking?"

It is interesting that we never read that they got lost. We want to know the destination before we take the first step. I wonder if God thinks, "Don't worry about the destination. I need you to take a step first!" Misstepping with God is okay. He works all things out for our good. He doesn't expect or demand perfection, just obedience.

We say things like this to God all the time. "I'll go, God, when you show me!"

And He says, "I'll show you when you go!"

I hope you have already established what it is He wants to do through the previous chapters. You know that God will be the one directing your steps, and that the Holy Spirit will anoint you to do it. There will be an ease about it, even though there will be detours and bumps in the road. You know the Enemy will try to discourage you and stop you. "I will give you every place where you set your foot, as I promised Moses." (Joshua 1:3). You are already promised victory before you even put your foot forth. Who else offers that? No one but our God. (I love Him.)

Remember the question, what would you do if you knew you could not fail? Do you realize you are promised victory? What a great God we serve.

In the lines provided below, write your prayer request for wisdom regarding the direction of your first step. If you already know the next step, write your request for success and further instruction. In Jeremiah 33:3, it states that if we call on Him, He will tell us great and mighty things.

_____

_____

_____

_____

_____

CHAPTER 12

COURAGE

Do you remember when you were a kid and playing took on a new meaning when you were faced with something that was going to require courage? Like the time I climbed up to the tree house for the very first time. There were four of us girls who discovered a tree house that our guy friends had built. It was impressive, and notably, it was high off the ground. There were pieces of wood nailed to the tree trunk that acted as a ladder and led to the secret hideout. We all wanted to ascend and occupy, but nobody was willing to go first and lead the way.

Finally, one gal mustered up her courage and took on that tree, step by step. When she made it to the top and entered the super neat hideout, somehow, one by one, we too found our courage and joined in the newfound treasure.

All of us girls wanted to climb the tree, but only one of us dared to do it. This is courage. This is what leaders do. They *do* what many want to do but don't, because they lack courage.

So the question is, how is your courage supply? Do you have what it takes to be the leader of this calling? Of course you do. Otherwise, God would never have chosen you for it. He doesn't call the equipped; He equips the called.

David had incredible courage. He faced lions and bears, and of course he faced a nine-foot giant. Where did his courage come from?

> David also said to Solomon his son, "Be strong and courageous, and do the work. Do not be afraid or discouraged, for the LORD God, my God, is with you. He will not fail you or forsake you until all the work for the service of the temple of the LORD is finished." (1 Chronicles 28:20)

Courage comes from Immanuel, God with us.

If God be for us, who can be against us? The answer is no one. We know this. The problem is we don't believe it. Not this again, disbelief.

Isn't it sad that with every twist and turn of our lives, we wrestle with disbelief? I find it very frustrating personally. I do, however, find comfort in the fact that the disciples struggled with doubt during their entire three years with Jesus. If they did, I will.

These verse below are describing a time right before Jesus ascended up to Heaven, after His resurrection.

Here is one place that really causes me to shake my head at their lack of faith.

> Then the eleven disciples went to Galilee, to the mountain where Jesus had told them to go. When they saw him, they worshiped him; but some doubted. (Matthew 28:16–17 NIV)

The eleven disciples did three things according to verse 17. What were they? They saw, they worshipped, and they doubted. Do you not find that both frustrating and comforting? I do.

We also know that these eleven went on to change the world to the glory of God. Let us not be afraid of failure, but find courage to try. Step out. Go.

> And Elisha prayed, "Open his eyes, LORD, so that he may see." Then the LORD opened the servant's eyes, and he looked and saw the hills full of horses and chariots of fire all around Elisha. (2 Kings 6:17)

I, like Elisha, am praying that you will have your eyes opened to the God of angel armies that go before you, behind you, and around you. I pray that you will be strengthened in your inner man to complete the calling that is within you. I pray that you will find your courage in the Lord.

When we look at the physical, we will feel totally defeated. We will see we are surrounded and surmise that we don't stand a chance.

When we look at the spiritual, we will have courage. We will see that the Enemy is the one who is surrounded, and understand that he does not stand a chance. Glory to God. Greater is He who is in me than he that is in the world.

David declared that some hope in chariots but he hoped in the Lord. If God be for you, who can stand against you? To Joshua, God said, "Everywhere you are going to put your foot, I have already given you. Be strong and of good courage!" To Moses, He said, "I am with you."

Go ahead. Be the first one to climb up the tree-house steps and see for yourself! Others will follow.

In the lines provided, write a prayer that your eyes will be opened to the great cloud of armies that surround you, just like God did for Elisha. Pray for courage—you are going to need it.

_____

_____

_____

_____

_____

CHAPTER 13

MAP

Well (big sigh), here we go. Let's begin.

Wouldn't it be wonderful if you had a map? We all know that the Bible is our map. I do not want to take away one iota from the Word. I do, however, wish to give you a simple visual so that you will be aided in your understanding of how to pray your way through. So I have included an exercise to help you map out your journey.

Once you realize where you are, you will have clarity about how to pray. Jesus often times went by Himself to pray. If He did it, we should do to. It is here in the desperation that we pray prayers we may have never prayed before. I was raised to say rote prayers. It wasn't until I met Jesus in a personal way through accepting His work on the cross for my life, that I started saying personal prayers. Often times it was one word prayers, like "Help!"

Let me be clear in addition to courage, faith, and His anointing, it is prayer that holds these all in operating order.

There may be times when you feel like you have lost your way. No worries. God has not lost you!

This map will help galvanize your journey. Please take the time and cooperate with this little visual. It won't take long at all, and I promise it will be eye opening.

I am smiling that maps on paper are almost a thing of the past. We have satellite devices now, like GPS! The hardest part of this exercise is holding the paper the right way in the beginning. I have done this exercise with many people to test out my wording and it makes me giggle how most (including me) are stumped with the folding!

I'm a visual learner. If you are also, then this will help you as it did me.

First, you need a fresh piece of paper. Turn it so that the eleven-inch side is at the top. Fold it in half, bringing the eight-inch sides together. Then fold it in half once again.

Now open the paper up. You should have four wide columns, not narrow columns.

- At the top of the first column, put the word *A-ha!*
- At the top of the second column, put the word *Battles*.

- At the top of the third column, put the words *Patient Plodding.*
- Lastly, at the top of the fourth column, put the words *Heart's Desire.*

Please continue to cooperate with me—there will be revelation!

You will be making this map personal. After all, you don't want to follow *my* map.

In the first column, under the word *A-ha,* draw an image that represents a moment when you finally realize something. You know how in the cartoons, a lightbulb comes on over Wile E. Coyote's head? You could draw a lightbulb. Make it personal. If the lightbulb doesn't work for you, choose something else that means something to you.

In the second column, under the word *Battles,* draw your favorite fruit. Put a couple of them in there. Also in this column, draw something that represents conflict, battle, and giants. There is a lot of action in this column! If there is any space, fill it with more fruit. This column should be full of drawing.

In the third column, under the words *Patient Plodding,* please put lots and lots of footsteps. That is all—just footsteps.

In the fourth column, under the words *Heart's Desire*, draw one big heart with a smiley face *in* the heart.

This completes your map. Now go do good things for God that will make people want to praise Him!

The End.

Funny, right? Of course it is! Look at this map. It just doesn't make sense at all. Honestly, when your *A-ha* moment happens and you dare to tell someone about it, they most likely will look at you the way you are looking at your map: a "Yeah, right" kind of look.

Without explanation, this map makes no sense. But it will make sense once I explain.

Your life may feel like that paper looks, but God wants to explain some things. Above all, He wants to explain who He is. Let me say that again: more than anything in the whole wide world, He wants to reveal Himself to you.

God's destiny for you is Him.

Do you really think you know all there is to know about Him? This journey will not only be a discovery of who you are in Him, but, first, who He is.

> My eyes will watch over them for their good,
> and I will bring them back to this land. I
> will build them up and not tear them down;

> I will plant them and not uproot them. I
> will give them a heart to know me, that I
> am the Lord. They will be my people, and I
> will be their God, for they will return to me
> with all their heart. (Jeremiah 24:6–7 NIV)

That is His hidden agenda. Let's look at the map. All the spiritual giants of the Bible would look at this paper and say, "Yep. Been there, done that."

You see, all of them had a calling, an *a-ha!* All of them had trials and battles mixed with the fruit from the Promised Land. All of them had a season of desert wandering that might have lasted years. And all of them fulfilled their callings.

The only transportation across this map is by faith. Without faith, there will be no forward motion.

Hebrews 11:1 reads, "Now, faith is confidence in what we hope for and assurance about what we do not see." This is what the ancients were commended for—their faith.

All the biblical giants took very similar routes. Through their obedience, God orchestrated life-giving concepts for us to follow. We have an audience cheering us on, as we read in Hebrews12. They tell us to run this race set out for us.

Here are the written explanations for each section of the map:

1) *A-ha!* is clarity in calling revealed.
2) *Battles* are departures from the regular routines of daily life. They are sojourns in this new pilgrimage. They are excitement of vision while confronting doubts. Here will be many tests by human circumstances and demonic threats.
3) *Patient Plodding* is travel through lands where fulfillment of God's promises is divinely tested. It is the desert period of believing in the Word alone. Tenaciously press through one step at a time, believing in who God is, overcoming obstacles.
4) *Heart's Desire* is Conquering in the Promised Land will have battles, but victory is promised with every step.

The *a-ha* moment comes when you realize what it was you were handcrafted by God to do, as found in Ephesians 2:10: "For we are God's handiwork, created in Christ Jesus to do good works, which God prepared in advance for us to do."

I am aware that I may have readers who are seventy years old or older and who think their *a-ha* has got up and gone. Let's read what Moses would say to that:

> "And the Egyptians will know that I am the
> Lord when I stretch out my hand against
> Egypt and bring the Israelites out of it."

> Moses and Aaron did just as the Lord
> commanded them. Moses was eighty years
> old and Aaron eighty-three when they
> spoke to Pharaoh. (Exodus 7:5–7 NIV)

Yes—if you have a pulse, He is still doing great works within and through you. Your age does not disqualify you. I daresay it solidifies you.

I believe that when we do the thing we were called to do, it is *incredibly* fulfilling. One might say, "Well, of course it is fulfilling!" Yet those who have walked in the last column would say it doesn't always *feel* fulfilling. For example, being a mom often does not feel fulfilling, and yet it is what I am called to do. People who are already in their calling sometimes fail to realize it because they use feelings as their guide and not faith. *A-ha!* Honestly, many of you have completed the journey before you even start.

Let's use stay-at-home moms as the example. For many moms who have chosen to stay home, this is their calling; they simply have not embraced it. One reason they fail to do so is because homemakers are often made to feel that it isn't enough, that they should be doing more than that. No, don't believe the lies of satan, don't get distracted from your calling.

Once someone grasps that God has given them the desires of their hearts, they can start experiencing fulfillment without the guilt. They can more fully embrace it, experience

God's favor over them, and produce even more amazing fruit for His glory. I personally think homemaking is one of the highest callings. Embrace it. Pray over it, expecting people to give God glory over your calling.

Jesus is our great example. He was called to be our Savior. He did not "feel" like dying on the cross, and yet the Bible says that for the joy set before Him, He endured the cross. For many, you are already doing the thing you would do if you knew you wouldn't fail. You simply fail to realize you're doing it! (Again: *a-ha!*) Perhaps you are being awakened to that fact. Once you embrace this calling, you will sense fulfillment like never before. A newness will give birth to joy amid your circumstance. You will be more focused and not distracted by the ever-present, "there has to be more to life," nagging Tempter.

Some readers will say, "I don't even know my *a-ha!*" Eureka! You now know your location on the map. Therefore, you now know how to pray. You need to ask the Lord for vision.

For those struggling with their *a-ha*, let's skip to the fourth column for just a moment. Scripture says He gives us the desires of our hearts.

> Trust in the Lord and do good;
>> dwell in the land and enjoy safe pasture.
> Take delight in the Lord,
>> and he will give you the desires of your heart.

Commit your way to the Lord;
>   trust in him and he will do this.
(Psalm 37:3–5 NIV)

See how He tucked that verse in between some instruction? We get the desires of our hearts when we trust in Him, delight in Him, and commit our way to Him. He will bring it to pass.

The *a-ha* moment is tied to your heart's desire. Let me be clear: there is a vast difference between head and heart's desire. Rarely are the two the same.

Once again, let's insert Moses into our map as an example. Envision him in the *A-ha* column. God spoke instruction to Moses from a burning bush. Moses' calling from God was not well received; Moses argued with God about His choice and why Moses was not the one to do this. Moses cited his speaking disability and certainly did not embrace this calling with joy!

I am quite certain the memory of the murder he had committed was commanding him not to proceed. He told God, for the most part, that He had the wrong guy. However, God knew more about Moses' heart's desire than Moses understood with his head.

Moses' head reasoned with this calling; however, God was calling to the depths of Moses' heart. Let's read Exodus 2:11–13.

> One day, after Moses had grown up, he went out to where his own people were and watched them at their hard labor. He saw an Egyptian beating a Hebrew, one of his own people. Looking this way and that and seeing no one, he killed the Egyptian and hid him in the sand. The next day he went out and saw two Hebrews fighting. He asked the one in the wrong, "Why are you hitting your fellow Hebrew?" (NIV)

What stands out to you in these verses? Is it the fact that Moses was moved because of the injustice done to his "own people"?

What is it about Moses' heart from his past that God is now calling him to do?

Are you *a-ha*-ing? God called to the depths of Moses' heart, to his heart's desire. God knew that Moses' heart was tender for his own people, and Moses' people were in need of someone to lead them out of slavery. Years of mistakes and traveling in the wrong direction were waging war on Moses' mind. That's why he told God, "No! You have the wrong guy!"

Like Moses, your *a-ha* moment will be outside your comfort zone. It will be bigger than you. It will require you to depend totally on God. If God doesn't show up, you are done. Because if this were something you could do, then you would get the glory. Scripture says that they will see my good works and give God the glory!

If the Holy Spirit is moving as I know He can, you may need to stop here and ponder in your heart like Mary did when she got news that she was pregnant. She was created to carry the Messiah! You know her head had to be questioning that one. But look at her response to the angel: "'I am the Lord's servant,' Mary answered. 'May your word to me be fulfilled'" (Luke 1:38 NIV).

This may be a good place to stop and ponder what the Holy Spirit is saying to you. Just be sure to come back— we have a lot of work to do!

For the person who just isn't sure yet what it is he or she is being called to, then your first step is to pray for the *a-ha*—for the lightbulb to come on, so to speak. Pray that you hear.

Let's read 1 Samuel 3:10.

> The Lord came and stood there, calling as
> at the other times, "Samuel! Samuel!"
>
> Then Samuel said, "Speak, for your servant
> is listening."

Perhaps He has spoken and you simply are not listening. If this is the case, pray for hearing ears.

When I go to the mall and I want to find a certain shop, I look for a directory. Once I find the shop I am looking for, I then look for the "you are here" *X* that tells me where I currently am. When I have the beginning and the end, then I can proceed in my journey.

Once you realize your calling (you are here) is tied to your heart's desire (your destination), you are ready for the journey!

It could take minutes, hours, or years to hear the call. I think the attentiveness in your listening may be linked to how long it takes to hear. We need to listen like our lives depend on it—that abundant life found in John 10:10.

Not that long ago, I had a mammogram. The doctor's office called, and I was told they had seen something of concern and I had to go back to the office for another test. I went the next day and was told the results would take a few days.

While the technician administered the ultrasound, I watched her eyes intently as she looked at the screen, and I listened to the sound of her voice as if she knew something she wasn't saying.

When my phone rang days later, I noticed the number, removed myself from the company I was currently in, and listened to the test results like my life depended on it. Because it did.

And so does yours. Your spiritual life depends on hearing God's voice.

(I am so thankful that the test results showed no further cause for concern.)

I have learned that as I walk with God, He talks softer and softer. He simply refuses to raise His voice over the busyness of my life. He bids me to be still and know that He is God. He will not compete with the lifestyle I am consumed by.

Is the same true for you? Do you find yourself asking God to bless your to-do list that He has not ordained?

His goal is not your destination. His goal is that you learn more of Him through the journey to your destination. Ultimately, that destination is heaven, our home.

This calling is bigger than your abilities. Again, you may have a desire to parent, but you will find it is far bigger than your abilities. When I had my first child, I was dependent on God. When I had my second child, I thought I knew what I was doing. Except this child was totally different from the first, and again I found myself totally dependent on God. Certainly when the third child came along, I was beyond confident about this parenting thing. As you might expect, this child too was different from the preceding two. All three of my children did life differently and by different stages.

This calling of motherhood was indeed my calling. I wrestled with the nagging thought that I should probably have developed a cottage industry and made millions in addition to my calling. False. Because of that doubt, I am not sure I embraced my calling as fully as I could have.

You get the chance to do it right the first time.(*A-ha!*) It is bigger so that God will get the glory, as you will be totally dependent upon Him. As you travel, you will get to know Him more and more. It's a great plan, a great journey, and a great God.

I have talked about stay-at-home moms quite a bit as an example, but what if God is calling you to be the president of the United States? Or to start a group home for single moms based on biblical principles?

Think small with intensity and think big with wonder.

If you have gotten this far in the book and still can't grasp the *a-ha*, you are in great, great company. Don't be dismayed. Abraham set out for a country and he had no idea where he was going. Take a step of faith and pray. Ask God to show you this life you were created for. Pray for your *a-ha*.

If you now realize you are already in your calling, then embrace it. Jacob had an awaking, let's read;

> Jacob left Beersheba and set out for Harran. When he reached a certain place,

he stopped for the night because the sun had set. Taking one of the stones there, he put it under his head and lay down to sleep. He had a dream in which he saw a stairway resting on the earth, with its top reaching to heaven, and the angels of God were ascending and descending on it. There above it stood the Lord, and he said: "I am the Lord, the God of your father Abraham and the God of Isaac. I will give you and your descendants the land on which you are lying. Your descendants will be like the dust of the earth, and you will spread out to the west and to the east, to the north and to the south. All peoples on earth will be blessed through you and your offspring. I am with you and will watch over you wherever you go, and I will bring you back to this land. I will not leave you until I have done what I have promised you."

When Jacob awoke from his sleep, he thought, "Surely the Lord is in this place, and I was not aware of it." (Genesis 28:10–16 NIV)

This Jacob is the one you know from the phrase, "the God of Abraham, Isaac, and Jacob." Jacob's grandpa was Abraham. If anyone should have sensed God, you would think it should have been Jacob. Read verse 16 again. He didn't realize that God was in this place. He was awakened. I am praying for your awakening.

For some, you are pregnant with a life calling. Think about what it is like to be pregnant.

At first, you may be happy or sad about the results of the test that shows this life. You may be in disbelief and entertain thoughts of abortion. You may rejoice and want to tell everyone. You do not look pregnant. You may have morning sickness, or extreme fatigue and body aches. You haven't felt life yet.

Oh, but you will. You will grow and make plans, creating an atmosphere for this life that you have been gifted with. You will change the way you eat, think, and sleep. You will grow and become uncomfortable with an intense urge to push—but please be careful not to push before this life is ready to be pushed!

Your water will break without consulting you and command your attention. You may labor for what seems like forever. When that life finally arrives, you may too tired; others will have to help you embrace it. This life is the most amazing life you could ever have been given, handcrafted just for you.

> For we are His workmanship, created in Christ Jesus for good works, which God prepared beforehand, that we should walk in them. (Ephesians 2:10 ESV)

Pick Me! Pick Me!

In the lines provided, write a prayer regarding what you learned today and what you want to ask of and/or say to God. I am praying that this will be a super sweet time with Him.

_____

_____

_____

_____

_____

CHAPTER 14

SWEET TUSSLE

As we cross over the bridge to the *Battles* column, you should consider enlisting people whom you trust to pray with you, and perhaps gently hold you accountable. It is here you may be tempted to retreat or quit.

As you can see, the *Battles* column is filled with fruit. The fruit represents the goodness of destiny. Do you recall the story of the ten spies sent to scope out Jericho? Joshua and Caleb reported that the land of Canaan was full of beautiful fruit and flowed with milk and honey. *But* (don't you hate that word? It negates everything that went before it), there were giants in the land. Big ones. Really, really big ones.

Yes, it was true there were giants. The eight other spies did see the fruit too. However, the giants seemed far greater than the fruit! All the spies saw the same giants, but not all had the same perspective. Don't let people who do not have your same perspective talk you out of this calling.

Everyone in the Israelite camp got riled up because of the eight spies who did not think God was enough for this victory. Fear filled their hearts so that Joshua and Caleb were outnumbered. Joshua and Caleb had a "but" also: Joshua said in Numbers 14:9 "Only do not rebel against the LORD. And do not be afraid of the people of the land, because we will devour them. Their protection is gone, but the LORD is with us. Do not be afraid of them."

Sadly, the fear won out. As a result, they experienced forty years of desert life. Keep in mind the original journey was an eleven-day journey. Grumbling and complaining turned the eleven days into a forty-year journey. Even though Joshua and Caleb believed that God could, they had to wonder with the others for forty years. That kinda stinks, doesn't it?

Joshua and Caleb were the only two who went into the Promised Land from the millions who did not. Sobering thought, just two from the original people got into the Promised Land.Let's learn from those two, believe in the land with giants and great fruit, that God is enough for victory.

I love what God said to Joshua when they were finally going into the Promised Land after all those years: "Have I not commanded you? Be strong and courageous. Do not be afraid; do not be discouraged, for the Lord your God will be with you wherever you go" (Joshua 1:9).

This is such a powerful, victorious promise? The above verses make me want to praise Him, even before the victory occurs. Praise is how you will get through the *Battles* section. You are going to have to praise your way through.

The Enemy hates when God receives the glory. Hates it. Remember when Jesus was in the desert and Satan tempted Him to bow down and worship him? The Enemy took his best shot at Jesus, and worship was on his top-three list.

We can surmise that if the Enemy wants worship that much, he will stop anything and anyone who produces people to worship God. This *Battles* part of the map shows that you should expect it. *But*! God is with you just like He was with Joshua and Caleb. And everywhere you are going to put your foot, He has already given you. I suggest you put your praise music on and keep walking through this part of your journey.

The Promised Land doesn't mean easy possession in God's agenda; it took thirty-seven years of battling once they were in! We don't often think of the Promised Land being such a battlefield, but it was. You will have things come at you to thwart the plan of God for your life. Don't be afraid or dismayed. God will fight every single one of those battles. You just remain focused.

In Proverbs 31:25, it says that you can look to the future and smile. When the battle sirens flare up and the rocket's red glare threatens your view, engage your faith eyesight and look to the Author and Finisher of your faith. It will produce a smile. We are more than conquerors. Think about those things.

Jesus always has a way of keeping us going, a "fruit" reminder perfectly placed to keep us going on the journey. I love that about Him. He guides so well. When you realize you are in the *Battles* part of the journey, you will have a greater understanding of how and what to pray for.

Here are a few things I learned along the way of my journey that you may find helpful.

Not every open door is necessarily a door you should go through, and not every closed door is a permanent roadblock. Listen for God's voice and walk by faith, not by sight. Test the spirits and let the peace of God have the final say on your foot placement. The walls of Jericho were huge! And there was two of them—that's right, not one but two. They fell, and your roadblocks will too if need be. Praise Him with a shout of victory.

Another thing I have come to learn is that doubt is my biggest threat to victory. It's as old as sin. Remember when the serpent tempted Eve and said, "Did God really say?" What if Satan only had one shot at Adam and Eve? He went with Eve because of her influence on Adam, and he used doubt. Boom, sin entered the world.

Doubt is a killer. Is your faith small? Is your faith the size of a mustard seed? Good; let's move mountains. Smaller than mustard seed? Pray for more. Pray and praise your way through. Walls have been known to come down.

The last thing I will share that I have learned so far is this: I didn't share my calling with everyone. I didn't give the Enemy an opportunity to have people discourage me. People can do that without realizing it. My biggest struggle was with the idea that God would use a waitress to encourage others to do great things. But as you can see, I wrote this book with the power of the Holy Spirit. I didn't need people's facial expressions to add to my own doubts. So I shared with very few, especially in the beginning. When I became confident of my calling, mostly toward the end, I opened up to more people, but not a lot. It still feels weird. But I don't walk by feelings; I walk by faith.

He is a God who rules His kingdom by peace. Think about that. Doesn't it seem that most kingdoms are ruled by force? I think of all the castles I visited in Europe. All of them were constantly being captured by force. God does not operate His kingdom like those of the world. He reigns by peace. Is it any wonder we are drawn to Him?

In this journey, we will have trials, all of them are producing things in us to make us perfect, not lacking in anything.

So when James, Jesus' brother, tells us to consider it joy when we encounter various trials, I think James is speaking from a place of deep knowledge of Jesus that we just don't know—yet.

Jesus said in John 16:33 "I have told you these things, so that in me you may have peace. In this world you will have trouble. But take heart! I have overcome the world."

Jesus is the overcomer, not you, and that gives us peace.

I don't know about you, but I like knowing the end of the story. It helps me relax through the rough parts. His Word says that, before you even sense a storm, you can know you will get through it.

Have you had bad days before? Sure you have. Have you ever had really bad, awful days? I can say confidently that everyone has had them, and everyone's success rate is 100 percent for getting through bad days. Everyone reading this has had a bad day—a trial, a storm—and has survived. You may have been bruised and perhaps injured but you were not destroyed. I love that God is still making good things come out of those bad days. That is how awesome He is. He is a great bad-day fixer.

I am providing some space for you to write a prayer regarding *Battles*, perhaps some that you have come through or one you are currently going through. Perhaps you are frightened about the fact that there are battles on your way to and through the Promised Land. Write out your prayer to Him. Pray and praise your way through.

_____

_____

_____

_____

_____

CHAPTER 15

ARE WE THERE YET?

Here, in the *Patient Plodding* part of the map, you will need constant encouragement and prayer accordingly.

When the Israelites had crossed the Jordan over to the Promised Land, Joshua instructed one leader from each tribe to go back and retrieve a rock from the middle of the river. This rock was to be a reminder for generations to come of God's faithfulness. I find it interesting that Joshua was specific that it should come from the "middle" of the river.

Isn't true that the middle of our journey is one of the most likely places to quit? Think about it. You have lost sight of the shore and the destiny is not in sight. Nothingness equals quit.

Stones of remembrance were important then, and they are important now. There will be times when you struggle to believe forward. This is when remembering backward is good. God is so faithful: He was then, He is now, and He will be tomorrow.

God has never let you down. If you feel He has, you may need to go back and get some healing in that area. He is a Redeemer. It is hard to trust Him forward with pain from the past that needs healed. You can't do anything about the past, but God can if you let Him.. He is such a great God and He loves you so much, He sent Jesus to bind up broken hearts and set captives free.

It is very possible that the many footsteps in this map will require some retracing. In order to move forward, you may have to move backward a step or two. I know do-overs are frustrating. Repetitiveness is sometimes exhausting, and it can be hard to stay enthused. Pray for renewed strength.

I have talked with many people that simply refuse to visit the past where they were hurt and receive their healing. They would rather press on and ignore the hurt they feel, refusing to deal with the pain. Often when I ask them how it's going for them, they say, "Not well." Yet they refuse to go back and get healing. Ultimately, we can get stuck there. I don't get that. God is good and would never lead us into a place to harm us. Why would we refuse? I guess they just don't believe He really loves them. Or they don't trust Him, mostly because they don't know Him well enough... yet.

If you are one of these people, if there is an area that has not been healed by the Healer, will you allow today to be the day to let the Healer in?

It was in the *Patient Plodding* section of the map that I gained healing. I felt like a failure most of my life. God could not bring me into my heart's desire with all that baggage. I had to purpose in my heart and take another step, believing that I could do this thing He was calling me to do. It was His Spirit in me doing the work and not me, I walked by faith while my feelings screamed otherwise. I talked to myself a lot in this wandering part. "I am more than a conqueror." Step. "I was created to do things that will cause others to give God glory." Step.

I wrote and rewrote chapters, feeling like a fool. I fought battles in my head that what I was doing was embarrassing and I would suffer embarrassment to publish such a thing. I had had to say things like, I am being called to be obedient and to trust Him. And then simply keep walking, keep walking.

I often think of the Israelites in the desert for forty long years. Can you hear them at year twenty-four, saying, "Didn't we pass that tree four times already?"

In this portion of the map, there may not be a lot of forward movement toward *Heart's Desire*, but there will be a lot of changes within your heart. Remember how I wrote that God's goals are not our goals? That His desire is that you know Him more? Well, it generally manifests itself in these countless footsteps.

In the desert, God usually does His best work. I know this personally. When all you have is Him, you realize that He is all you need. This is great revelation. Oh, sure, we hear that, we say that, but when we really experience that, it is soul satisfying. For when we delight in Him first, then He gives us the desires of our hearts.

Forty years is a *long* time to be in a desert. I laugh at how much I pack to go camping for four days. I can't wrap my mind around desert life for forty years. And the packing up and moving again whenever the cloud or pillar moves! On this journey, you are going to have to drop the baggage of life and lighten the load. You don't need it; it simply will wear you out.

I am quite certain I would have perished in the desert from grumbling. I am so thankful I am on this side of Calvary and His grace is abundant toward me.

And while His grace is wonderful and available, we have a great responsibility not to misuse that grace. We actually have a greater responsibility now, on this side of Calvary not to grumble in the desert while we are plodding, because of the price that was paid.

God is the same yesterday, today, and tomorrow. The things that upset Him then upset Him now.

When the Israelites grumbled, it was because they were self-focused. "What about me? what about me?" God provided every need they had, every single day. Food, water, and shelter, every single day.

The truth is, the Israelites *chose* not to go into the Promised Land, that is a hard truth. *They* failed to believe that God would give them the victory in Jericho. They couldn't believe forward, because they failed to remember what He had already done. Leaving Egypt was a wonderful however, it was short-lived in their minds.

> For whatever was thus written in former days was written for our instruction, that by our steadfast and patient endurance and the encouragement drawn from the Scriptures we might hold fast to and cherish hope.
>
> Now may the God Who gives the power of patient endurance (steadfastness) and Who supplies encouragement, grant you to live in such mutual harmony and such full sympathy with one another, in accord with Christ Jesus. (Romans 15:4–5 AB)

Did you catch that? Encouragement is drawn from Scripture. You are going to have to be in the Word, like a fish needs to be in water. Your encouragement is found in God's Word for you.

In the desert, you are going to have to take your Bible reading to another level. If you fall down, you should bleed Scripture. Perhaps He will want you to set up camp somewhere in the desert for years. Maybe not, but He might, and you are going to have to be okay with that. Otherwise there isn't going to be much joy, and there will be the danger that grumbling may occur.

I have heard it said that waiting on God when you don't know why you are waiting is one of the hardest things to do. I think I agree. Ask Sarah. She struggled with waiting. When God didn't come through on her timetable, she took matters into her own hands, and we all know how that turned out.

Don't get tied up in doing good. In due time, you will reap—*if* you faint not.

You have got to believe that God will make this happen. When you are on the backside of the desert and it is taking years, you are going to be tempted with all the Enemy has. Will that be you? Are you a quitter? Or are you in? Are you going to agree with the Holy Spirit and be all that God has created you to be? Or are you tempted just to coast through this life and wait for heaven? Will you hear the words, "Well done, good and faithful servant"? Will you remain faithful to His calling?

I think you will do this. That is why I didn't give up writing this book. I know that God is speaking to a generation of people who want to be all that God has created them to be. I didn't give up in my six years of desert, and you aren't going to either. We both want God to be glorified in our lives. So let's keep taking that next step. Then, the next one. One more. Keep going; you got this.

Pray for strength for this journey, strength in your inner man. You are going to need it.

_____

_____

_____

_____

_____

CHAPTER 16

SUPERNATURAL

I would like to share my story. Perhaps you may be encouraged. I was very focused on becoming a professional golfer in my early twenties. I had everything in place. I had a coach who had two gals who were already on tour. He was the pro to the pros at Walt Disney World, he was the president of Club Makers of America, and he was coaching *me*. I lived in Florida and was golfing every day. I worked as a waitress for my income and was completely focused, no distractions.

One day while I was getting my lessons, my coach got a call and had to go into the clubhouse. This was long before cell phones! While I was waiting for him to return, I had a strange thing happen. I had the most intense urge to get married and have children! "What was *that*?" It left as quickly as it came.

"I don't want that," I said. "I am going to be somebody someday. I don't have time for that homemaker stuff." I was driven to get on tour. Irv, my coach, came back, and I never thought another thing of it until years later.

I could spend two more chapters filling in all the details of how the years played out, but I won't. I will tell you that I never finished that golfing dream. Today, I am still a waitress, I am married to the love of my life, and I have three daughters, amazing young women of God.

The day that Irv took that phone call, the Lord interrupted my hyperfocused golf lesson to give me a wakeup call. He gives us the desires of our hearts, not the desires of our heads. God knew my heart way back there, all those years ago. He knew that what I truly wanted was a husband and children. My head was so driven, I thought what I wanted more than anything was golf.

Looking back on it, what I really wanted was for my dad to notice me. *Pick me! Pick me!* has always been the cry of my heart. I wanted my dad to pick me over all the things he choose that came before me. My dad loved me, but unfortunately he was rarely home. He played golf. I like sports. Subconsciously, I think I believed that if I went after a career in golf, then maybe my dad would want to spend time with me.

I wonder who else out there is longing to be noticed and picked? Who else would say, "I am living my life just to get attention"? Sometimes we can do really crazy things to get attention. As children of God, we must cease this craziness. He is the God who sees us. Hagar named Him El Roi—the God who sees me.

There were many opportunities for me to continue with professional golf. However, there was no peace in my heart to pursue it. I could have shrugged it off and done what my flesh wanted to, but by the grace of God, I did not. I wrestled with God in my head for a solid year. My heart only found peace when I patiently waited. I had no idea what I was waiting for.

Until one day, a man named Steve walked into my life, and I have never been the same. Steve became my husband and later the father to my children. I would rather have Steve and my daughters than a golf career. I can say that now, here in the Promised Land. I did not see it that day on the driving range. Jesus spoke to the desire of my heart that day, even though I didn't fully understand. I didn't have a map, I didn't have a mentor who knew the ways of God speaking into my life.

I struggled with letting my dream go. I felt like my worth lay in what I was trying to achieve. How could being a waitress be anything special? I wanted to do something big, do something great, not be a waitress.

But being a wife, being a mom, being a waitress, feels natural to me, like I was created to live the life I have been living. I have no regrets, except that I wish I had known then what I know now. If I could go back, I would embrace this calling with passion and zeal.

Don't believe the lie that you have to do something famous to have worth. Do things that make His name famous, that is praise worthy.

It is my desire that people will read this book and respond to what the Holy Spirit is saying to them. Just like He infused my golf lesson that day, I pray that He reveals to you what you were created for. I pray that you will embrace it and give God all the glory.

Before you were born, He had a plan for you. I pray you will be awakened to the freshness of it, that you will embrace it, and that you will be moved by it.

I envision people who have been in their callings and have never realized it before. Now, with the help of this book, they will embrace it and go full steam ahead to walk this path with such intensity that others will praise God as a result of their lives.

I see people doing wonderful things, like walking in complete restoration with their pasts, turning around and daring to believe that they can help others with the very same struggles they have been set free from.

Some may have realized that they are pregnant with a dream, and with the help of this book, they have felt life for the first time.

For all of us, the next step seems scary and exciting at the same time. It has a supernatural feel to it. Go ahead, believe.

He has chosen you. Respond to His calling.

Now let me pray for you;

Father God, it is my turn to pray for those reading this book. Please increase their holy hearing and holy sight to walk this path that you have set for them. Surround them with people who will encourage them. Remove the people who would discourage them. Give these precious lambs of yours a hunger for Your Word like never before. Breathe life into their lives by the power of Your Holy Spirit, the life You sent Your Son to die for—life abundant.

I am asking You to help them choose this life. Increase their faith. May all who read this book of encouragement complete the work You have set before them, so that they may hear "Well done, good and faithful servant" coming from Your lips to their ears.

Thank You, God, that You use people like me. Thank You, God, for using people like these to make Your name famous. Jesus, thank You for giving us Your name to approach and make our requests known.

And so, Father God, it is in Jesus' name that I complete this book for Your glory and make this request for those who dare to believe also. Amen.

May God bless and bless and bless your life.

Go be all God has created you to be.

AFTERWORD

This book came about while I was teaching an adult vacation Bible school one summer. We were reading a book by Henry Blackaby called *What's So Spiritual About Your Gifts?* This book really challenged us to move out of our comfort zones. It was a call to listen to the call of God.

Truly, you should read Blackaby's book. It stirred me to act. So why the need to write another book? Because I believe I was the only one moved that week, and I am not content with that.

This book has a soldier mentality: to leave no one behind. I understand the struggle to believe. I am committed to encouraging everyone who will dare to believe a mustard seed's worth that perhaps God is talking to them. I want to encourage the littlest, most broken, most overlooked, most forgotten, most neglected, most abused people and tell them that *they* have been chosen. God longs to make His name famous through *them*.

The love of God compels me to write about the calling of God just one more time.